The River Painter

The River Painter

Poems by Emily Grosholz

University of Illinois Press Urbana & Chicago

Publication of this work was supported in part by a grant from the
Illinois Arts Council, a state agency.

Acknowledgments

The Hudson Review: "Letter from Germany," "The Metaphysicians,"
    "Galerie Orphée," "In the Light of October," "Aux Balcons,"
    "97 rue Compans," "Dinner in the Courtyard," "In the Garden,"
    "The Last of the Courtyard," "Petition for the Trees"
The Kenyon Review: "Reflections on the Transfinite,"
    "The Dissolution of the Rainbow," "Marathon"
The Bennington Review: "Ode to the Senses," "Egon Schiele's
    Self-Portraits"
Cumberland Poetry Review: "Woolgathering," "Ithaka, "On an
    Album Leaf," "Birds, Trees, and Lovers"
Poetry: "The River Painter," "Gathering of Friends"
New England Review: "The Return," "On the Balcony"
The Iowa Review: "In Medias Res"
Harper's: "Edgewood Park"
The Massachusetts Review: "Following the Dordogne"
The St. Andrews Review: "On the Ferry, toward Patras"
The Black Warrior Review: "Rodin to Rilke"
Calyx: "On the Loss of My Mother's Jewelry"
South and West: "Ruins at Jumièges"
Connecticut Artists: "To Cathy"
Prairie Schooner: "Crescent Moon"

Library of Congress Cataloging in Publication Data

Grosholz, Emily, 1950–
    The river painter.

    I. Title.
PS3557.R567R5   1983   811'.54   83-4875
ISBN 0-252-01098-1

This book is printed on acid-free paper.

To My Parents,

Frances and Edwin,

In Memoriam

Contents

Gathering of Friends, after the Fall
of the Sung Dynasty

Bamboo, rock, and tall tree, by Ni Tsan

Four friends got drunk together late one night.
The talk, the waning hours,
the cavernous yawn of the moon through the window,
the wine and the color of the wine
intoxicated and ignited them.
To mark their celebration
the host unfurled a roll of silk:
one by one they took the brush,
mixed up the ink, and wrote
what their hearts bid them write.

The first one's slurred but graceful hand
set a tree ingrown like a will denied,
fisting itself against the wind;
then added four dark lines of characters,
crows in the sky calling their names:
we are the unvanquished black-haired race.

The next added a shadow of bamboo,
which wind lays flat against the ground
until it blows itself to breathlessness;
straightway the muddy leaf
stands up again to flourish at the sun.

The third put up a drunken line,
a staggering array whose sense
and flow described the party's history:
how they were all consoled, then overjoyed,
then overflowing so they had to let
their feelings take expression in the brush.

The last one placed a rock
in the low corner of the page,
to hold the painting down to earth,
to fortitude, for all its play.

His conclusion in the end was just:
their play came to its point

in the substantial courage of the flesh.
They were a soldiery of ink and brush;
I say that any man is equally brave
who can confess he loves his friends,
gives himself up to love of wine,
draws out the secrets of his heart
and hangs them up in black and white. . . .

Especially when outside the wing of night
engulfs the moon; bad fortune everywhere
plays with the bones of men; unearthly war
casts his red eye and brandishes his sword.

On an Album Leaf

by the Chinese Painter Ma Yuan

Two sparrows in their plume
composed like folds of silk
ride on the quiet brim
of a long leafless waterfall,
branches of the willow tree.

A sage wrapped in his winter cloak
approaches through the snow,
thinking perhaps of other snows
in threescore years and ten,
of cherry blossoms, the long passage down.

His feet upon the frozen bloom
make not sufficient sound
to rouse the sparrow or its mate;
but once he comes to stand
beneath the willow, gazing at the sky,
he meets the sparrow's eye.

The silken eyebeam twists,
draws thin, and breaks. The pair
desert their dry cascade
for the securer sky,
achieving easily the tiered
pavilions of the air.

The River Painter

In the winter, after the new year,
Chao Meng-Fu paints the river
to recollect himself.
The long line of the river bank,
the pale of snow or distance in between,
mark out his journeying
from one year to the next.
He tries to call back who he was
at the last stopping place,
what face he discerned in the water;
his eyes change color
from blue to gray to green. . . .

Once, gazing, he lost his visions
in the jaws of an ancient fish.
"Fish! Myself! I must recover. . . ."
The old fish only laughed
and plunged back, its eyes tarnishing,
into the mud of the river bottom.
Chao Meng-Fu painted that river scene
again and again, the circles on its stream
and the fish at its heart invisible.

But in the spring he lifts his brush
only to give himself away,
to lose himself, betray and fly.
For spring is not the time to save,
but time to sow seeds up and down
the river's edge, leaving oneself
in cloudy paper skins always behind.

It is the time to venture forth,
when earth itself is scattering
its seeds and wings, is letting
blood into the swelling tips of trees,
the buds that fill and rise
to touch the inner chambers of the sky:
scarlet, hot to the touch, about to bloom.

Then Chao Meng-Fu is master of his brush.
Placing it, just once, from here to there,
he in his godlike gesture recreates,
creates for the first time the river bank.
He becomes, like a god, at one
with his desire, and the line,
like the trace of a god,
is only himself, thrown off
with a god's abundance.

That painter lives his vocation better than I.
He throws off silk-skins like his art
with easy grace, and travels by his brush.
He carries out his journeys on the silk,
by the true shape of trees, black rock by rock,
as I set out in word by word
mere promises to take myself away.

He makes the stream unfold
just as a reader's fingers turn the scroll,
making the landscape open, the river flow,
the small boat drift on the waves;
and the dream of spring come home
straight to the heart: blue river scents,
the sirens of the flowers, irises,
light flowering among the young bamboo. . . .

Chao Meng-fu writes out his art
in black and white, with ink and brush,
in images as plain as characters;
his means are no more rich than mine.
Yet that puritan calligrapher
can carry out the spring, himself ride
transport of leaf and wave toward his desire;
like a god in his image, divine
his own leave-taking, as at the scroll's end
in empty silk, the stream
becomes the great dispersion of the sea.

The Voyage Out

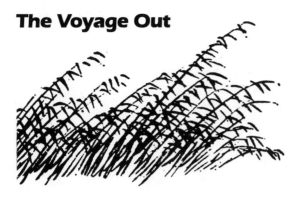

Dinner in the Courtyard

When summer tears the maple leaves
to lace, and blue shows through the green
like those imagined distances
weaving through all things close at hand,
then sunset looms for hours upon
the scarlet tenements of day,
unraveling curtains, windowpanes
ablaze. The house is close, I say,

and move the table underneath
the arches of the maple tree.
Not even the curious neighbors know
if I am host or stranger here,
nor if this roof of leaf and air,
the little courtyard of the world, is home.

97 rue Compans

A spot of color! said the white-haired
gardener, her scarlet fingernails
mauve with black dirt, her lipstick's red awry,
tamping limp geraniums in a pot
whose handles were the ingrown horns of satyrs.
I admired her industry,
but never was really sure about her motives.
Why did she dress so brilliantly to garden?
The courtyard throbbed a little in surprise
at its heart of darker green,
the barren lilac, maples and ropes of ivy
where spiders hung their wings in cotton foils.

The landlord's son, who oversaw the courtyard
to work without abandoning idleness,
appeared sometimes with a bottle of *Ricard*
and warmly encouraged Madame Labiche's progress
among the potted flowers.
In fact, he must have fallen in love with her
despite the uneasy difference in their ages.
Though he never declared his affection,
he chopped off every lilac one day in April
and presented the lavish bouquet
to her confusion and everyone else's disgust.

Some people quickly forgave him,
discounting his reckless act as a crime of passion.
But whenever I saw him taunt his timid wife
or send his children out to buy him liquor,
I found it hard to suppose
his romantic, because impossible, heart's desire
excused his various flurries of unkindness.
Besides, he often forgot or misplaced our letters
(Madame Labiche's he opened), poisoned cats
instead of the swarming mice,
and persecuted the roots of the maple tree
which rose beneath our feet like a buried star.

Souvenir

I keep returning to the days I spent
on the other side, behind the Buttes Chaumont,
to half-remembered, ordinary things:

Shopping along the rue des Pyrénées
for tiny shrimp, translucent coral and gray,
bouquets of aerial pinks
I carried like a cloud, glitter of petal
and violet shadow.

Under cover of evening
I quit my books and mounted boulevard
and alley to the courtyard—tired, breathless,
pushing the heavy portal.

By the rue des Solitaires
I keep returning to the same high ground
above forgetfulness, above
the crowds of Paris.

I pushed the gate and always
met the children spinning out their play
around the tree of heaven,
Hesperus and Venus, as if the star
of evening ran beside the star of love.

And you stood in the doorway
framed with ivy vines, the scent of olive
and garlic on your hands. So I came in,
smiling, hungry, bearing my gift of wine.

On the Balcony

We understood at last the native tongue
of the candle struggling to maintain
its story on the balcony, in the wind,
set opposite the quiet moon.
We felt ourselves grow darker with the wine
and an increasing reticence
that waited near us like the sleeping children.

Perhaps it was the music playing
deep inside the rooms behind the wall,
blues from south Chicago with no words
but those the flame supplied,
curved and falling like the wind in veils
or flights of stairways down,
a failure and advancement, always down.

Perhaps it was the blind wall with its traces
of ivy, advertisements, empty rooms,
pattern of our two dark heads by moonlight
broken by the candle's shifting tongue.
All our talk became a listening
and echoed from the wall
in letters and the seams of vanished stairs.

The moon, the candle, answered to each other;
we heard the small one gutter
in imitation, loving and unstable,
mocking and shaking, of the silent moon.
We listened till we half believed
it was the language of the dead,
their strange flat hands like ivy on the wall.

So distracted by the task of living,
we must turn for wisdom to the ones
who wear the past upon their faces
as the walls of houses do,
as the moon reveals itself in phases
moving from a scored white vacancy
into the baleful silhouette of fire.

We watched the flame embrace the wax,
the crumbling wall surrender to the touch
of ivy, sinking deeper in its scars.
Close behind, the music played,
the children slept enfolded in a dream,
their respiration like a lower
run of minor notes, descending scales.

Later the flame dropped off, so suddenly
we wondered, drunk and silent as we were,
why our light companion fled
and left us to our old abandonments.
Your darkened face, just after, lit
to features I could understand;
I read it with my mouth and hands
because my eyes were full of night.

In the Garden

Where are the children?—Sido

Up in the hazelbush that stood for a tree
at the southmost wall of the garden,
the children lived like swallows
while their father and I cut grass
underneath, and weeded and watered the yellow roses.

They climbed by swinging up on pliant limbs
and imagined a different home,
disposing all they owned by pieces of string
on the branches around them:
dolls, bells, bags of raisins, water bottles.

Parts of the house became a constellation.
The children quarreled, sang and fell
on the hill of half-moon grass
we gathered underneath them, plash, unbroken
as falling stars against the roof at midnight.

They rose and fell, delighted,
walked up the stairs of grass into their tower.
Although they never learned to fly,
they overarched the swallows easily
with their continuous invented music.

But where, where are the children?
I've been to the house and garden
lately, alone; the bush has tassels,
the garden is overgrown, the swallows
repeat their single note among the branches.

Perhaps the gypsies stole them.
Perhaps they've found another home.
Perhaps they'll come to light again next spring
when swallows travel back from Egypt,
nesting in the ships which still have sails.

The Last of the Courtyard

Who will believe me later, when I say
we lived in a state of music? Passing birds
and mice met on the roof, and danced away.

Francis played his silver flute, and Guy
his violin; the children sang in words.
Who will believe me later, when I say

we lived on little else from day to day?
Life in the courtyard was its own reward.
Mice danced across the roof, and ran away.

Carpenter, painter, potter: poverty
is the sole good a singing man affords,
though not at last sufficient. As they say,

we lose the things for which we cannot pay;
our houses were sold out, over our heads.
Even the dancing mice must go away,

nothing remains of us but memory,
a fleeting minor air, absently heard.
Who will believe me later, when I say
the mice danced on the roof, and ran away?

Petition for the Trees

The courtyard at 97 rue Compans, valuable property near the center of Paris, was sold to developers, and all the inhabitants were evicted. This message was left behind, written on a wall of one of the small houses:

To the new owner:

In this place, whose walls breathe quietly, whose windows filter the tranquil light, where the trees grow suspended in the patience of time; here our children lived and played, families of painters, sculptors, and artisans. . . .

Even though your interests now lie in destroying and emptying the life of this place, Monsieur, don't attack the trees. Look up at them for awhile, let them overshadow you. Then, from the threshold of hope I say that they will still be standing when you and I are gone.

Aux Balcons

The rue Ménilmontant runs up a hill
to meet the fading neighborhoods of Belleville,
all destined to perish soon
beneath the city planners' printed blue.
For weeks I lived up there without you,
rooming in a hotel called *Aux Balcons*
whose balconies were nothing more
than curly grillwork fitted in the windows.
Mornings turned my window to grisaille
whenever the Paris sun laced through
the clouds and iron flowers.

I hung up blood-red oranges from Spain,
Indian scarves you sent me long ago,
maps of the Aegean and rough brown apples
against the speckled walls.
The room looked out behind all my disguises,
admitting its shabby furniture again
in the full-length looking glass
which now and then, on my scattered reflection,
posed the curves of your half-naked body
between its silver surface
and the mercuric window of the sky.

Poetry, mathematics, streets and dreams:
books became another kind of romance,
leaning toward me on the slanted shelves.
I worked against the future,
kept two candles burning on the table
so I could go on reading late at night,
and when they drowned at last in their own eyes
I read the shapes of darkness.
Solitude came down at intervals
like moonlight on the wall,
creating its own sweet time, another life.

I ate my dinner at the window, watching
traffic coiling through the streets of Belleville,
raucous and exotic as the aisles

of some North African bazaar.
And over that harsh variant of silence
I listened for your footstep, sometimes
opened to an empty entryway.
Sometimes I set a candle in the window
intending to bring you home
so I could fall asleep, as if you were
the true illumination of my dreams.

II

On the Ferry, toward Patras

Corfu appears, and then the distant blue
draws her away again: uncertain hours
as time begins to drown in voyaging,
no talk, no books, no breakfast taken late.
The sea, divided, falls behind the boat;
I see that blue laid back on darker blue
the way Odysseus must have, when his mind
was emptied of its cleverness at last
by ten years' wandering. His thoughts are mine,
an island without houses, flocks, or trees,
undressed of all its causes. Memory
slides by like waves against the running prow.

What memories could wake my tiredness?
The clothes upon my back, unspoken words
I always carry, wounds from an embrace
too often entered, now are all I own;
along my flesh I feel them hardening,
a frieze that tells the future as the past
and scrolls my progress roundly on my breast.
I cannot keep my secrets to myself.
I am the figure of the ship, and where
I've traveled, where I go, what I will do,
assail and tear aside the simple blue.

The Island Philosopher

Poros

I

You stayed on the island's darker side,
away from town where streams
of tourists ebb and flow.

You too lived staring into
the gold mask of Seferis' poetry,
listening behind the hollowed eyes
for voices of the dead.

With solitude at hand
like a cistern's yielding blackness,
you wrote from underground
books whose pages dried to white.

If there was a girl in town,
her name was Absence or Silence,
so beautiful you took her only at night
when you could not see her face.

II

I have made love to solitude, like you,
night after night. How many times
I turned upon my bed
trying to touch each one of the sensual planes,
temple, breast, and thigh,
all three dimensions melting in my hands.

Ringed by books, I let
the engine of my mind rage on at sixty
as I sat moveless, marrying
one thought against another;
great, fleshless couples left and right,
every velocity I hit
skidded against their images.

Distant now, your face appears
on the inverted mirror of my eye,
the turned dark side,
the backward of the moon.
A filament of terror runs across it
like the silver lightening my hair.

Crescent Moon

Light disperses over the small church
set high against the cliffs, the arch
of triumph delicately incised
with spirals of acanthus
and Roman angels carrying the hours.
Swallows circle, and the moon appears
to my surprise and sadness, here,
just as it does beyond my windowsill
at home.

      Tracking an absent poetry
in limestone walls, bleached lavender,
skies which whiten at the close of day,
I came because it was the season.
Pilgrims go on pilgrimage
out of a curious or true desire
to see the dead one's bones and fingernails
in southern places where the sun
sets late to give another hour of light.

These relics, undeniable, belong
to one who like his creatures perishes.
See where he goes down once again
beneath the ivory cliffs, and from
his latticework of flesh
a rib, still luminous,
displayed by feathered spirits, starts to rise.

Over the Abyss

You went back alone
to your deserted hillside
and your box of colors, searching
for the blue that binds
and lets all other colors sing.

Between the olive trees, the pines,
this woman and this man,
the void resides; it severs
even the ethereal bodies of air.
In that prism of emptiness
only light can find a place,
carrying on its secret life
which we, intent on things, seldom discern.

But you must see it in between
the pines, who study to dispose
the spectrum of its elements:
russet, brown and blue,
cousin to irenic gray,
a dozen greens beside the green
worn by the pine itself.

You analyze the fields, what hides between
mint and lavender,
shaking children from the skirts
of that Madonna Misericordia,
unraveling her bands of violet
for color and for scent,
as gently as you turned on me before.

Then won't you also discompose
the nothing between rock and pine,
between your face and mine,
which now the metal ruler of my plane
so sadly, so precisely measures out.

Draw from the luminous honeycomb
gold that moved the Byzantines

beyond the strict embrace of space and time.
On your hillside, all alone,
unlock the house of blue and gray,
paint the broken sides
of every single thing:
let the peaceful colors have their way
and gather all the sundered creatures in.

Katerina's Garden

Who will paint the drunk
pistachios behind the house
where Katerina lives?
Trunks of silky blue,
green leaves, orange fruit,
Kabuki trees that twirl
and bow, as she walks by.
They reel beyond the frame
of her poems, too well known
to name, for they are hers.

One of her Parisians
will take their likenesses,
a stranger who rents out
the lefthanded cabin
beside the mastic trees.
The yellow eucalyptus
stands like a soul,
veiled, imperturbable,
no matter how he suffers,
and he does, in the cold wind
November carries in
from the slow Aegean.

The pine and the fig tree
reckon up their fruit
like two old fishermen
in the village at noon,
exchanging histories
over fried fish and ouzo
when the catch is in.
The painter sits near them
staring out at the sky,
and Katerina tries
to draw his cold figure
back into a poem.

He shivers at nothing.
Against the twofold bole

of an olive tree he covers
a woman's form in black,
breast of silver, waves
of hair coiled to her waist,
shadow fast in leaves,
sky filling the hollow
blue of distances
where her heart should be.

In Medias Res

The whip of pleasure sends us all,
our sensitivities bright red,
delighted, lightly nipped, to some extreme.
Herodotus observed that at the edge
of the recorded world things grow more strange.
Hot spices and monstrosities
are carried in by camel to the center,
where civil, solid folk are pleased
to pay a lot for something from the corners.

Thus we who cannot travel very far
but in imagination, sometimes fall
deeper into the boundaries
than tourists like Herodotus, who saw,
made notes, and came away
all the more Greek for what they thought they knew.

Hard at the center, we undo
the casks of Scythia and the serpent Nile,
plunging through crimson, musk, and wine
to find what we are dying to,
our secret folded there among the spoils.

Galerie Orphée

Now in Olympia wild carrot snows
the disenchanted temples.
Judas trees put on their scarlet flowers
and slowly let them go;
tourists trample the dwarf irises.

But in the little hills
where cypress are a balustrade
on stairs for no one, asphodel
display their white existence undisturbed.

My friend, returning from his winter travel,
opens his shop again for the new trade.
He carries marble children near the door
so they can see outside,
removes a bronze Medusa to her corner,
hangs the paintings in a row like windows,

slowly, with the same familiar gestures.
Through the painted windowpanes
I see him, but my voice has disappeared
into another dialect of silence.

Truly, what could I say?
The endless contemplation of the past
which travelers and lovers carry on,
though natural, is idleness.

Not all our errant ways,
the skewed inertial line of history,
can move beyond the compass of the flowers,
nor slip from the embrace
of Immortality, that bitter woman.

III

Marathon

Across the green which lifts and falls
like ocean, like St. Mark's mosaic floor,
whose gilded earth the sea buckles and swells,
turning on Venice that same supple force
she used to trouble other shores,
her lion-headed ships her battering ram;

across the green, how far the runner sails,
spread out against the wind, his legs
impelling earth until the earth recoils;
or tacks without an effort through her hills
as easily a sailor on his girl
sets out at night to bring his vessel home,
slapped by the waves that rise and fall for him,
the lunar tide that sends him into port.

Perhaps he finds a current, and gets on,
arriving at Bermuda in an hour;
perhaps a northerly and toothsome wind
diverts his path, drives his tormented blood
to circle like a whirlpool in his heart;
he never has the leisure to prefer.

The voyage that he runs will never end
as long as time suspends him in the green:
his limbs fail, and are mended one by one;
his heart breaks, and is filled again; his bones
throw tendons, which like vines rewind
about their bole; his nerves fire off and on.

He always runs, through tearful hurricane
or Indian calm; his steps are westerly;
the sea swells like an untimed heart, and he
rocks like a little ocean in the sun.

Augurio

Rome, November

Green capitals, acanthus spirals
underneath the high invisible
ceilings of the Domus Flavia,
and wintercress still thrives
in the Farnese Gardens.
Harsh weather never arrives,
and I would love to settle
in an old quarter of Trastevere
by the Via della Scala.
Rooms with a fireplace burning
olive or bitter laurel,
incense for winter gods who bring
roses and bougainvillea,
not the cold fantasies of snow.
One window on marble stairs
that mount the tangled green
Janiculum, one window listening
to a fountain in the small square
where I'd descend each morning
to the neighborhood bakery;
my dark-eyed man makes coffee,
hot chocolate for the children
quarreling like swallows in the ivy
before they go to school.

And then I'd go off too,
tracking the sixteenth century
beneath the frescoed skies
of the Corsiniana or Angelica.
Strange country of old books,
where words like *vinculum*
link substance down the page
to causes, hierarchy, back to god,
our reasonable imaginings
that things and forms embrace.
Is this a human binding
or the book of the world? At dusk

I skirt the traffic, carrying
trout and fennel, wine,
garlic and studded potatoes home
for supper. The children nod
at their lessons, the fire sings
antiphonal to the fountain
and Santa Maria's chime,
its flickering tongues describe
a forest on the walls
of ilex and twisted pine.
We are left together, gold
and pale as painted gods.

Ruins at Jumièges

I cut across the buckles of the Seine,
up the steep slopes a mile to level ground
half circled by the deep
white channel of the stream;
through forest, fields, and down
again to meet the river. Cherry trees
on every hand covered their red in green,
while men on ladders pillaged at their hearts.
I left a trail of cherry seeds behind,
though no one followed as I passed,
my bicycle as trackless as the wind.
So far from what I mourned, and should have feared,
I fled with more than Normandy in mind,
more than the river in my eye and heart.

An ancient abbey stands in Jumièges.
The western towers, twin battlements
against the tides of darkness, still remain,
but every wall is gutted, overgrown,
and the high roof, the paradigm of heaven,
is long since stormed away.
Between the nave and choir there is no stair,
no screen to keep the crowds from their desire.
Only a copper beech, the prince of trees,
whose monumental bole could bear
the manifold thin nervures of the air,
divides the floor. The leaves divide the sky
in panes of bronze which fan
around a spectral cross of red and green,
so the lost vault becomes a sheer
translucent window, and the blue between
the blue of distance, as it ought to be.

I came to stand beneath the broken height,
and listened to the birds who did not sing
but flew like angels, portioning the sky
in principalities, dominions, thrones.

I mourned for what was lost,
well lost, not knowing that my heaven
was dust already, scattered at my back.
The wind grew stronger, scattering the wings.
I turned; my step was blind and halt;
the vaults above shifted and fell, a stone,
a leaf weighed on my thoughts. I should have known,
passing through the low walls alone
from ruined paradise, not by the door,
the serpent at the heart of all
that love had offered me.
I walked out blind, not knowing where I was.
Not yet, not then; the light studded the trees,
but the dark branching shadows, what I'd lost,
the evening tide, was all that I could see.

Voûte Nocturne

Baudelaire walked in the evening
down the Ile St. Louis,
past starred lights in the Seine;
watched the stars change place
like birds in the chestnut trees,
watched the starlings light
and cover their eyes with their wings.
What was he doing there?
Thinking about his mistress,
looking for something high or low
to compare to her darkness.
A poet is always walking out
to find an emblem shaped
like his passion, with a name,
for his passion has none;
passion only bears
a poet's words away
in a race of foam.
When Baudelaire looked down
into the dark, descending Seine,
did he see the sky's face
blackblue with distances?
his eyelid's purple vault
when love shakes and escapes him?
the shadow of his mistress
when she passes beneath him?

The Poet and the Canal

Dem Dortmund-Ems Kanal gewidmet

Canals run through a city
at a level deeper,
straighter than the welter
of superficial streets;
carry out a slower,
longer train of thought.
Daytime, full of barges
trafficking like minutes,
fleeting and as frequent;
socialized by families
of ducks and swans, who flaunt
round their mechanical
great cousins, brilliant
steerages and rotaries.
Families of people,
most often on Sundays,
come out in demurer
formations, but as colorful
and thick of plumage.
Banks stocked with fishers
are richer in dreams
than signs of fish;
the lines lead under
uncircled surfaces
sharp into fathoms
of speculant green.
At night the canal is
never so populous.
Waterfowl hide
and drowse at the edges;
the fishers have fled
to their upland houses.
Still, darkened barges
are tied by the shore,
the stars in transit
appear on the water,
trees by the towpaths

use the wind's voices
to speak to each other.
Then the canal's
univocal flow
is deeper and clearer
to late-night walkers
who pause to hear.
Let poets recall
canals to the busy
forgetful city:
how through its surface
of pain and confusion
that quiet channel
runs like a vein.
Lively but orderly,
with some commercial
uses but better
productive of dream.
Just a flight down,
open to anyone
who takes the stairs
contrary-wise,
that low domain
our troubled higher one
always sustains
and underlies.

To Cathy

I stopped in a forest
of thin white birches
today, at sunset.
Their silhouettes
wore only foliage
of flattened clouds,
stamped with gold,
lettered by branches.
Dear correspondent,
I wanted to send
so fine a message,
but it was hard
for me to decipher.
The silky light,
or the characters
both white and black,
or the calligrapher's
longing slant
filled me with tears
till would I or not
I couldn't see.
So I send this letter
instead, to say
I wish you'd been there.
You who have clearer,
intenser vision
would know why I stared
and saw no farther;
your absence stirred
and curbed my powers
of transliteration.
So now I send
a different version,
truer to loss
than to satisfaction,
the longing slant
blindly expressed
in character, hand,
design, and word.

Letter from Germany

Though it is only February, turned
less than a week ago,
and though the latitude is upward here
of Newfoundland's north shore,
Mother, spring is out. It's almost hot,
simmering above and underground,
and in my veins! where your blood also runs.
The hazels dangle down
green flowery catkins, and the alders too,
those bushy, water-loving trees,
have a like ornament, in purple-red.
Spring is so forward here.
Snowbells swing in garden beds;
the pussy willows that you liked to bring
inside, to force their silver fur,
are open in the air;
witch hazel in the formal park,
still leafless, wears a ribbon-petaled bloom
of yellow and pale orange.
Once or twice I've walked through clouds
of insects by the river to the east
of town; the ducks are back on the canal
now that the ice is gone, loud and in love.
I wish that I could bring you here
to see this fast, unseasonable spring;
I wish that I could write a letter home.
But since a year you are not anywhere,
not even underground,
so that the words I might have written down
I say aloud into the atmosphere
of pollen and fresh clouds.
I say the litany of my desires,
and wonder, knowing better, if you hear
through some light-rooted organ of the air.

The Return

I

Ithaka

Now it is one to me, and I don't mind
letting myself fall open to become
children, the vase of love, another essay
toward philosophy unformalized,
poems with no fixed habitat.
It doesn't matter, since the world
resumes the place left empty,
taking on the shape described
by nerves and girders, ribs and walls,
collecting the light-worn substances
our skeletons must somehow draw around.

I don't mind thinning into monotones
of wind, an empty tree,
flute-bones of a bird that lost its way
in March, caught in the middle of its song,
a note, a rush, a nothing. The exchange
is fair, the world allows
a hundred versions of equality.
Whatever source decants, the hollow
conches of a fountain, wells again
with water, leaves, the passengers of April
reinvested with their wings and song.

I don't mind filling out with memories
of emptiness, a yellow sail
once belled, collapsed and silent in the hull,
or following the routes of pilgrimage
to marble ruins which refuse
our praise and send us home again
to bury the white form of traveling
beneath the kitchen door,
as if it were a hound that waited
years for us, and died just at the hour
we recognized the sign
that says, no farther, here
your dreams lie down.

Woolgathering

Caught on combs, forks, the crooked
elbow of the armchair, startled gloves,
ivory ribwork in my grandmother's fan:
what is this half-stuff which settles down
around the house on quiet afternoons?

Snow, I think, except it doesn't
melt, or crystallize in symmetries.
Dust? It never hides itself
in corners. Breath? It rests unlike
the busy wax and wane
of human inspiration.

Perhaps the shamble-footed sheep
with wide black eyes
like those of lovers in the dark
leave it behind; it reeks
of lanolin and clover.

These are the sheep I dream
as I lie reckoning,
awake, my vacant hands
before me in the air,
drawing some new matter out of nothing
with the fluid gestures of gathering.

Spring Fever

At the wood's edge trillium shows
mauve petals in three,
blood-root fragile white
planets down the ecliptic of the road.
I can do nothing better with my eyes
than seek the early risers out;
my self rides up and down,
teased from sterner purposes
by love and evolving spring.

Too restless to stay fixed
at my desk, which faces city streets
through windows darkening
with dust and spiderwork,
I ride my bicycle by morning
out to country at the city's edge.

I never touch the violets,
Quaker ladies massing in their dress
of blue and white, the common pinks
ignorant of their family's Latin title.
Empty-handed, given to pastoral,
by night I ride back to my lover's bed,
trailing names of flowers from the woods.

Birds, Trees, and Lovers

Trees once suddenly learned the art
of flowers, and inherited the earth,
we say, inventing time;
and birds have colonized the treetops
ever since their silver scales
divided, flared and lifted, mastering
gravity, we say, keeping the books.

But neither the ornamental tree
nor birds in the radiant sky
oaring from island to island of brown
blown crown of branches, take
their place in our bookish time.
Perhaps because they are always perishing
or because they live forever,
paradigmatic crest and braided wreath.

Indeed, my love, since human lovers began
to read the clock or compass of the world,
threading their way through the forest
of symbols with clever hands,
they have liked to compare their splendid
pleasure to bird and tree,
reflecting on the solidly feathered diamonds
perched in golden crowns above their heads.

Daimons, they say, we seem to be
always perishing and always perfected.
But they are deceived in their wishes,
forgetting that human romance
is a genre of history.
For when they walk out together, they never move
in a circle, but arrow hard
through the tree's heart, and the house
of the unschooled, musical birds.

Edgewood Park

In Edgewood Park, the flowers bloom like souls
for Dante, haunting the swampy meadows where
I soaked my shoes, along the little river,
under the bridge, beside the dusky woods.
The latest loosestrife withers, jewelweed
is hung against the darker side of winter,
sumac has turned scarlet, mint leaves bitter,
Queen Anne's lace to seed, carelessly scattered.

Autumn again; my dearest friends have scattered,
seeds out of their houses, lovers flown
southward to the heart's own Carolinas.
Things could be no different; such harsh changes
had to be worked out to the last measure.
Summer's instrument is cast and broken,
my song spelled in dust, the empty flowers
given wholly to their lineage.
The wings are long dispersed, the seeds are sown.
Close to the edge of my life's latter age,
I am surprised to find myself alone.

Letters from a Gardener

October 7

Do you wonder where I am? As the fates have it,
those long-fingered weavers, I find myself
in the northern mountains of New Mexico.
Life suddenly came to an end in California,
at once too comfortable and dangerous,
where lotus-eaters bloom on every corner.
Ten months ago I came to give a talk
on orchards to a group of farmers here,
and found the Bodhi needed a new gardener.
It's taken me ten months to turn my mind
from California, but finally here I am.

Six acres on Jemez Creek, which runs between
the constellated hot springs of the canyon;
at night in the autumn air, now growing colder,
I sit beneath that other milky way
alone, in water hotter than my blood.
The place belonged before to Benedictines,
buildings mostly low, built of adobe:
large community kitchen, dining hall,
rooms for meditation, pottery workshed,
greenhouse, orchards, and outlying fields.
All day we hear the fluid sound of wind
through the by now half-golden aspen trees,
and lighter music of running water, winding
only a dozen yards from where I sleep.

What has always attracted me to Zen
is just the practice of living here and now;
desire for another, mystic world,
desire itself, engenders suffering,
and the iron ego is its driving wheel.
We rise at 4:15 for chanting, tea,
stretching, meditation, and then breakfast;
zazen again, a little time to think;

showers, hot springs, zazen, dinner, time
to be alone; zazen and tea; lights out
as the other lights come on in the cold evening.
Write when you can. Much love to you, amiga.

October 22

You see, the Bodhi's not a monastery;
though we were lately visited by thirty
Japanese Rinzai monks, none of whom spoke
a word of English—they all carried cameras,
shot rolls of film, and bought out every piece
of the Bodhi's American Raku pottery.
They presented our Roshi with a bronze of Kannon,
a Bodhisattva; Roshi took them around
to Taos, Santa Fe, and Colorado.

Sasaki Roshi, now almost seventy,
came to America fifteen years ago
to teach, at the request of his own teacher.
He is a rock, whose center of gravity
roots him to bedrock. He can see right through you:
sanzen, the personal interview with Roshi,
must be the hardest thing I've ever done.

The aspen and cottonwood are blazing yellow;
the Bodhi garden is still full of flowers,
zinnia, cosmos, hollyhock, marigold;
and fruits: tomatoes, eggplants, carrot, onion,
melons, cucumbers, squash (winter and summer),
and chili peppers, soon to be hung up
as brilliant sheaves of red, in front of houses;
cabbages and Jerusalem artichokes;
forty fruit trees in their second winter.
We're opening some untilled land to grow
winter rye, first step in building soil;

the soil is mostly clay, redder than flesh.
Water comes from wells and irrigation.

I keep myself as open as I can,
attend the discipline of concentration
through faith that alters with despair, and hunger.
Already I've written too much; I just can't say
it all in so many words. You understand;
we suffer because of what we have forgotten.

November 23

West from my window virgin mesa rises
a half-mile over the narrow Jemez valley.
My favored haunts these days are pueblo ruins
up there, eight thousand miles above sea level;
I sit and muse in the home of juniper, cholla,
prickly pear cactus, ponderosa,
piñon and all the varieties of oak;
as well of rabbit, squirrel, deer, and elk,
bear, rattler, coyote, and mountain lion
visible sometimes at my eye's dark corner.

The sky is a deep blue, the winds are gusty,
fast-traveling clouds will briefly mask the sun;
warm days, cold nights, the coldest time of all
is the still interval between dawn and sunrise.
Only the Russian olives across the river
still hold their leaves; willow and elm stand naked;
raccoons come down at sunset to watch and bathe,
to eat the harsh, hard fruit the ash lets fall.
The Bodhi garden's all but harvested;
only Daikon radish, turnip, kale,
parsley, salsify, onions are in the ground.

I'm building compost, cleaning local corrals
and stables for manure, hauling in loads

of leaves and wood chips from an abandoned sawmill;
watching the fall-sown rye green the red soil
ever so slowly, making a cover for winter;
cleaning all the tools and machinery;
making an inventory of bulbs and seeds.
The Jemez pueblo is holding all-day dances
for corn and harvest; we may trade some chickens
for Hopi corn, squash, melon, gourd and bean,
chili pepper seed, and instructions for planting.

December 6

These December mornings we are greeted
by the late-rising and last-quarter moon,
walking across the dry grass to the Zendo,
where we drink green tea, chant from the Sutras.
How did I sleep through dawn so many years?
The lowered sun comes late into the canyon;
morning work has already begun
when light slips down the steep walls of the mesa.
Incense of burning piñon drifts from town,
a smell which belongs in essence to the pueblos,
especially now when winter lies on the land.

Weekends a caravan of pickups and trailers
brings wood to town, some cut on designated
National Forest lands, and some just deadfall.
Most families here have summer gardens, fruit trees,
chickens, and burn the gathered wood for heat;
but whereas once the houses were adobe,
pumice, stone, and wood, these days they're mostly
prefab or mobile, foundations all uprooted.
The Atomic Laboratories pay good money,
and when folks go up now into the mountains,
it's in an aluminum trailer, bought on credit.

The practice of clear-cutting lumber leads
to vicious erosion over the mesa slopes;

the fishy smell of money enterprise
wafts up the valley too, developers,
land brokers, marketing folly, greed, and waste.
We already live so well, but it is never,
for our American green-stuffed lusts, enough.

Tomorrow is the eve of Buddha's enlightenment
under the Bodhi tree, and so begins
a season of intensive meditation,
daily sanzen with Roshi, and studied silence.
Here I stop writing, caught in the spirit of things,
and wish you happiness for Christmastide,
my traveling companion. Siempre. Michael.

Following the Dordogne

It is so long, Sarah, this time my hands
wind and unwind, like the ribbon tangled
inside my typewritter; when I try to straighten
the turned sentences, my fingers blacken.
One letter on another darkens the page.
How much better to trace out the curve
of the Dordogne, as we did last summer,
counting off roses from our bicycles
beside the river, pure
because unnavigable.

Better to be working up the hills
that part the river valley from
the uplands: wondering if heart or lungs
would break at such crabbed epicycles, climbing
the highway tier by tier, until
we won the summit and the gentle grades
on the plateau, the bands of gravity broken.

The uplands were a different world,
set off above the lush, close-cultivated
patchwork of the valley, towns and gardens
full of tobacco and roses, their golden smell
of dust-motes hovering in the afternoon,
silenced against dank cliffs that held
the northern rain-clouds like a cradle
padded with moss, festoons of raindrop and fern.

The uplands were always spare, unwatered,
fields not clearly divided by low stone walls,
roadbed specked by rocks and the odd flower, pines
turned back and inward by the unbounded wind.
The earth itself turned outward as it mounted
the way a flower from its center opens,
so from our vantages we dreamed we saw
across the hills' corolla the dim sea
a hundred miles down south,
the blue of distance swimming in our eyes.

Up there the sky was clear, as if the clouds
had issued from the river, apparitions
visible only in the underworld
of the valley, narrow, fuming, blind with incense,
where even the longest vision is constrained
within a modest ambit,
so like the leap of heart within its prison.

Why sit still and wait until tomorrow,
feeding sheets of paper onto a spindle,
killing the beautiful whiteness with our labor?
How much better to leave nothing behind,
practicing freedom, the river on one hand
and limestone cliffs made immaterial
by the gold leaf of sunset on the other.
I loved the way we traveled, fast and trackless,
spinning mile upon mile
the great world's true appearance.

II

The Metaphysicians

When through circumstance,
steely accident, the world's rule,
lovers deny themselves the copula
of flesh, then it is true
that abstracter conduits
carry out the body's wish.
Atmospheres of breath,
direction of the eye,
words' intonation, fingers' drift
metamorphose
in the service of love.

Then everyday relations
grow erotic, extreme,
doubled in significance;
gestures, looks, and words
transfer as in a dream
the sense of one desire
into another. For we are
not creatures of necessity,
compelled to have or not to have;
pleasures we deny ourselves
may change in kind and keep, removed,
their pitch in a new range.

So restrained are you and I,
all our community
is just the globe of air
scored by musical designs,
our liason nothing more
than great circles drawn
and spanned by desire.
Still we discover
more than substantial charms
when our spheres coincide,
and the broken center swarms
with silent tumult suddenly
like the eye of a storm.

Between lovers in the flesh
distance at every stage persists,
and continues to divide
when the copula is made.
So the formal boundary of sex
which we have never passed
is just lovers' difference
made corporeal.
To you I swear, my body,
strictly beyond your touch,
only more and more
cleaves to the barrier
and is yours already.

Ode to the Senses

Aristotle trusted them, but the mechanical
philosophers saw all
too clearly what we must abstract from:
to the skeletons themselves!
Not the usual underclothes of calcium,
but a fretwork of hinges, valves,
and pulleys whose own elements
were sines and cosines, epsilon
and delta in the odd, ill-fitting garments
of shrunken triangles with empty sleeves.

The reasoners, enlightened by their reasons,
traded the great continuum of sense
for Euclid's empty spaces,
pure, unbounded, blinding, without direction;
filled it up with atoms
to which the senses could not come
in principle, and these moved up and down
like ghostly fingers on piano keys
of ghostly ivory, to the tune of some
increasingly harmonic function.

We are left with nothing to hold or view,
savor, scent, or carry near
the curious ear; no velvet solitude
of humming bees on honeysuckle vines
through which the sky turns yellow as the sun
descends, and carries lovers down
the surfaces of their desire
entwined with nerves and veins and tiny hairs.
Descartes and Galileo came to brand
such wisdom secondary, dreamed
by the body and not true, though good enough
for the dim wit of ordinary life.

What some had hoped, however,
that the beautiful and true

were linked in one sublime equation,
was at last made fabulous forever.
Guilty or saddened at this dissolution,
Newton tried to save appearances
by drawing all our motions under three
axioms and a brace of rules, our functions
underneath the bole of that white pine
which does not cast a shadow,
twisted like the arched neck of a swan
which neither swims nor sings,
nor feeds its little ones,
nor spreads its wings, the integration sign.

The Dissolution of the Rainbow

"By an extraordinary combination of circumstances, the theory
of colors has been drawn into the province and before the
tribunal of the mathematician, a tribunal to which it cannot be
said to be amenable."
—Goethe, *The Theory of Colors*

A cut-glass chandelier dangled above
the desk where Newton read and wrote;
all morning spectral dragons fought,
mocked him and made love
across the white wall opposite,
flashed their blue and sea-green scales, the fur
of tiny fires, a glittering red eyelight.
Then one day they suddenly
fled, and no longer were.

Rising in impatience, strangely lit
by reason, the philosopher undid
prism by prism the trembling chandelier
to run her now constrained and broken
offspring through a maze of barriers.
The light went through its paces
but the dragons disappeared.
What remained Sir Isaac quantified,
teaching Nature not to sing
her sweeter variations, but in one
low tone, geometry, to answer him.

Although white light is manifold,
a mixture, so he found, of different rays,
each ray could be identified
in essence with its angle of refraction;
this was the only origin of colors,
color then reduced to numbering.
The dragons lapsed to silence, mortified,
curled up and dry as worms a child
has questioned in the fire
of curiosity and left behind.

When Newton set his prism work aside,
he wiped his hands, and wrote on creamy paper

long and elegant formulae,
a shadow of the sensuous retained
in his illuminating study,
even that much immaterial.
Yet he sometimes noticed, later on,
how his sines and cosines lay
across the paper like dark skeletons
of dragon, couchant, rampant as the full
proud curve of the integral.

Goethe in Verona

I can't find it, he said to the almond-eyed woman,
and gave up his search for the day, rejoining her
on the highest terrace of the botanical gardens
which overlook the river around Verona.
But I have every reason to think it's here
on the Alps' Italian side, where antique flora
have always found protection from bitter weather.

He had been hunting that small, pale, almost leafless
Urpflanz, which is the childish grandfather of all
nature's overabundant bouquet, if it exists.
It was, he imagined, a kind of decorous lily
without lanceolate leaves and silver bells,
a true false Solomon's seal, that had no cause
or wisdom to discriminate itself.

Goethe stood apart from his companion
and watched the tumbled red roofs of Verona
changing to umber in the light's decline,
a little surprised at how his imagination
failed him, since it had long become his custom
to find what he himself put into nature
greeting their father like well-brought-up children.

The almond trees were just beginning to flower,
spangles of blue in the twilight, fair and scarce
as Hesperus and the other early stars.
The earth was not yet green, but the voice
of fountains sang in the last of winter's frost
and ten years' labor at Weimar. Little bats
like drunken birds went sideways in the air.

He felt he could trust the circle of his five senses
as long as he continued to practice green,
magenta, blue, and the complex strata of lines,
designing the very life of Italian prospects,
as long as the little *Urpflanz* kept
its peace somewhere, untroubled within a landscape
waiting to be discovered, touched and seen.

What else could he feel, who suffered so profoundly
the music, scent, and texture of coming spring,
the sheen of anemone and gentian, showing
colors barely unfolded above the sheath
of bract and leaf, like the Veronese lady composing
herself at the edge of sky and marble plinth,
her pearls the dimmer seconds of Hesperus?

Though Goethe knew very well that over the Alps
in Paris and London, the physicists of Europe
were fabricating a novel ghostliness,
the truth of an underworld beyond the senses,
he still beheld the failing rose of day
which drew itself across the terraced slopes
as the flower of light in blossom, not decay.

Rodin to Rilke

That sensualist Rodin, who used his mouth
and nose to sculpt, as well as hand and eye,
(his models too, traced lovingly as his clay),
said to the mystified young poet Rilke,
Work! Keep working, industry's everything.
More in works than words, Rodin declared
that once he'd loved the easy, lyric line,
nymphs flowing in a wave, or wings in air;
but now he took the harder, subterranean
labor of making his way into the earth
like a totem mole, a caveman, a digger of graves.

Trying to learn the paradigms of clay
he went for the gates of hell, not paradise:
worked up a crone, dry sticks and withered breasts,
Balzac fat as a steer, the Baptist, blind
and blackened by desert sun, mad to the world.
It's the body, the clay that matters, and secret death
like sex is the body's trophy. You have to get
down in the cave to work out the springs of man.
Black, damp clay is my master now, he said;
you see how it stiffens, fires to a beautiful red.

Egon Schiele's
Self-Portraits

Schiele drew the double of himself
before a full-length looking glass
which gave his backward image back again
faced forward, and twice framed
by the drawn mirror and the drawing's border.
His flesh is pale as paper,
bound by a fine line, his brow and groin
are darker; just the hand, astonishing,
and the sad blushing cheek are touched by red.
His second, with a lover's repetition,
echoes every curve and covers him.

Trying to break Vienna's charming circles,
set piece of façades and closed
Ringstrasse, Schiele broke the mirror.
So those one-way windows with their blinds
and casements never held
his image prisoner, the way
they must have if he were a creature
merely autoerotic, self-absorbed.
Instead, the crimp of hip evades,
the torn and lowered shoulder flows away;
the more his line perfected him, the more
his vision, flesh, and shame
were given over into other hands.

Shame, he scrawled across the broken glass.
In the slums, our own outlying districts,
children wail, their faces pale or blackened.
We who stand uneasy at the border,
staring at the artist's thinner body,
the second face depicted in the mirror,
find ourselves pressed close against the lover
just as if our hand traversed
his ivory chest and inner thigh, the place
that reddens at our question, cold and warm.

Once we have entered on the fine
disjointed curves, no choice remains
but to enact his vision, as the line
unwinds itself and coils about our arm.

Reflections on the Transfinite

Reading about the tower or great-boled tree
of ordinals, I think how Cantor grew
more wise and more insane, trying to save
his tree of Jesse from the pruning shears
and kitchen gardening of Kronecker;
though I must share the latter's feeling for
the natural numbers, those deceptively
well-ordered, step-wise creatures, which appear
transparent as they mount, but all in all
among themselves are most unknowable.

Dreaming about the cardinals, at night,
the alephs flaming like a candelabrum,
I see you in the attic of your house
installed between Diogenes Laertius,
nachgelassene Schriften, commentary
on Aristotle, Plato, and the latest
fashionable fact-shredders out of Paris.
So cloudy is the place you occupy
in the last hierarchies of my world
that I hardly discern you; yet I know
you are not just a postulate I made.

You are the great collection of desires,
forever incomplete, unsatisfied,
toward which all finite sequences in time
with little steps so trustfully aspire.
Though you outrank them all, see how they run
like atomies of fire toward the sun,
sent over the abyss with no alarm
to make the leap across into your arms.

Remembering the Ardèche

April plunges the classroom into light,
aisles of elm trees glitter beyond the window,
and I must pause midsentence, wondering
where you are. En route, no doubt,
chasing the easy skirts of camomile
along the Dordogne, south to Gascony;

while I remain suspended in my lecture,
fistfuls of wit cast before flocks of students
who long for the spring migrations,
chafing at their confinement from the weather.
I wear my patience like a light-green dress
and wear it thin.

It must have been in April
you and I walked together all the way
from Langogne to Aubenas,
never once meeting a window set in a wall
to sever inner from outer; only the high
clearstory of sunny clouds raised upon hills.

Allhallows

Flocks of birds along the Tussey Ridge
fly south: as our desires are leaving us,
as ghosts descend and take their names along,
the very current of forgetfulness.

Instinct drives the birds; they won't get lost
along the range of russet hills
that close us here, though some of them
will never make this pilgrimage again,
dropping from the air like rain
changed into crystal, shattering
their music on the granite shelves.

There are too many passengers
to name or number every one.
Surely a flight of chemicals
arrayed around a racing heart
has no use for a human name;
why should we mourn for them, those bells
chiming at the gates of speech?

II

Leaving work at five, we go
westward to the parking lot
where our cars wait: perfect, cold.
Light flares and slowly dies;
the bars are gold, then iron.

As our desires abandon us
like songbirds letting fall
ribbon, apple leaves and bits of straw
against the brown of autumn grass,
we watch them fly, half-blind,

recalling still the underscent
of silky nape and tilted knee,
the nest of hand and thigh.

What we most fear to see,
a woman's body in the shadows,
violated, faded,
is just the small gray sheath
of Philomela, feathers stiff
around her bladed song.

Each gossamer that passes
labors with a seed.
Beyond the veil of darkness,
disembodied, brood:
sing, tongueless nightingale.

In the Light of October

For V. G. M.

The long red seam across her throat
shows where her thyroid, instrument
of checks and balances within
the body's greater, delicate machine,
no longer lies. This afternoon,
the sleeve of light unraveling, she drank
a glass of radioactive iodine
to melt the last small edge
of poisoned tissue down.

Now for a day she radiates
in isolation like a minor sun,
closing the bedroom door to company;
and sits beside the window, looking down
on ranks of cattails autumn
thinned and scoured, the Sound's
blue mantle gently thrown
around the shoulders of the cove.

Her husband, for so many hours
unable to disturb her solitude,
sleeps and wakes in the cold living room,
imagining the rose
she plucked a week ago
from one late-blooming bush:
how radiant around a central gold
the shadows held like petals, luminous.

Flower of Grass

Dear teacher, now so far away in Paris,
I want to tell you what I've learned this winter
since you've been gone. I learned to love my father
again, although my heart still halts before him.
I found a river coiling through cattail marshes
whose banks I ran along, on icy snow
practicing to be stronger, more sure-footed,
and felt my lungs like wings gather the air.

I sent out dozens of letters; some discovered
their end, and some found whiter resonances,
returned to me like ringdoves, empty-handed;
my writing desk is thick with olive branches.
Like veils of light from truth's mysterious body
I've stripped off stages of chrysalis, only to find
countless more folded wings, some gray, some painted.

Love comes back as well, in flesh and in spirit,
leaving the bedclothes always in disarray.
Sometimes I strip the sheets and walk to the laundry,
delight in the sober order of winter cleaning;
or leave them simply undone in the morning, showing
the praise of disheveled hair, that love is chaos.

It is the conversions of lead into gold, of pain
to finer knowledge, and sometimes even to pleasure,
that commonplace, that tiny flower of grass,
I've undertaken to study through the long winter.
Your poems, invisible teacher, were part of my study;
your absence instructed me too, your letters awaited
which I read in imagination and kept near my heart.

On the Loss of My Mother's Jewelry

One ring was sapphire, ocean
in a circle of foam,
split diamonds. Another,
two drops of blood
rubies, a teardrop between.
As long as I knew my mother,
feared her, loved her,
her hands like emblems carried them.

Bracelets of solid gold, filagree
of leaf and stem;
necklace of little pearls, coiled gold;
brooches, pins with butterflies;
worn by her mother, grandmothers, aunts.
I have lost count
of all that was lost,
the old trove she left me in trust.

The box is empty now, like a mouth in winter,
not a pearl left, small as a seed,
no link of gold, gold dust, kernel of amber;
I have lost count
of tears shed and wasted.
The line of inheritance severed,
I never will wear again
these ornaments worn once on throat and hands
I loved, as I loved my own.

They are now laid by
in darkness which seals
lost things away, which covers
my mother as well.
Her life's treasuries
slipped from her early;
my loss is nothing to hers.
But where shall I lay it all up,
my corrupt treasure in heaven,
now that the haven is plundered?

What have her hands, emptied twice over, left me?
Memories, grief, regret,
she left me enough:
my life in its prime,
bright circle, with seeds
of blood dark at the center,
gold chains of tenderness, pain
deep blue in the heart's mirrors.
Blind eyes, look here, I still wear them.

To My Daughter

You are so small that shallow water
breaks above your shoulder; but you stand
straight with your feet in the sand,
frightened, delighted.

Your salt blood, blue-green
in rivulets beneath the skin,
draws you away from me;
you were the ocean's daughter
before you were ever mine.
I too, before you were born,
escaped my mother.

Little one, though you and I
hold ourselves hard against
the tide of that great river
rounding continents,
we are fluid at our center.

One day you'll take the waves
in your arms like a lover
as I do now, for hours
half in, half out
of that seductive element.

Oh ride forever on your diviner parent,
though I am long dissolved away,
ride over the crests, as white,
as fine, as wildly play.

The Return

"Abraham makes two movements: he makes the infinite
movement of resignation and gives up Isaac . . . ; but in the
next place, he makes the movement of faith every instant. This
is his comfort, for he says: 'But yet this will not come to pass, or,
if it does come to pass, then the Lord will give me a new
Isaac. . . .'"
—S. Kierkegaard, *Fear and Trembling*

The gesture of resignation
as the knight of faith
turns his hand like a calyx back
from the bloom on Isaac's cheek
shows that no illusion blunts his pain:
death lies on the rock.
Yet somehow Abraham regains
the life he laid aside: what floods
the empty circle of his arms?

The moon pulls back the waves
one by one from the sand,
lace covers quickly, hopelessly unmade
to yield the empty bed
of earth, the grave of love.
What radiance fills the place
from which the shining ocean fled?

The lover, lingering,
turns down the twisted sheet,
the last silk leaves of clothing,
hoping to see the other
shiver, warm at the root,
the blood flow back like summer.
But in the darker wake of love
each one restores the other, as they were:
here is your own, like Eve's
apple in hand. See, even the skin
is intact, with its luster and veins.

So the poet to her inventions,
so the mother to her child:

take, creature, your own true future,
its shape no longer moans and hides
in me, but wakes in you. And when that one
pulls on the globed
mantle of its own intentions,
what does the sad creator welcome then,
what rushes into the hollow of the heart?

Blind Galileo, father of the moon,
cheated of both telescope and eye,
what filled the dark horizons of your sight?
The dance of fire and stone
in order through the sky.

So the bereft, abandoned, blind,
cry to their lost inheritors,
go, you are not I.
The creatures flee and constitute the world;
the dance begins again,
the solid world, the moving world.
It is the world that enters in.

Poetry from Illinois

History Is Your Own Heartbeat
Michael S. Harper (1971)

The Foreclosure
Richard Emil Braun (1972) .

The Scrawny Sonnets and Other Narratives
Robert Bagg (1973)

The Creation Frame
Phyllis Thompson (1973)

To All Appearances: Poems New and Selected
Josephine Miles (1974)

Nightmare Begins Responsibility
Michael S. Harper (1975)

The Black Hawk Songs
Michael Borich (1975)

The Wichita Poems
Michael Van Walleghen (1975)

Cumberland Station
Dave Smith (1977)

Tracking
Virginia R. Terris (1977)

Poems of the Two Worlds
Frederick Morgan (1977)

Images of Kin: New and Selected Poems
Michael S. Harper (1977)

On Earth as It Is
Dan Masterson (1978)

Riversongs
Michael Anania (1978)

Goshawk, Antelope
Dave Smith (1979)

Death Mother and Other Poems
Frederick Morgan (1979)

Local Men
James Whitehead (1979)

Coming to Terms
Josephine Miles (1979)

Searching the Drowned Man
Sydney Lea (1980)

With Akhmatova at the Black Gates
Stephen Berg (1981)

More Trouble with the Obvious
Michael Van Walleghen (1981)

Dream Flights
Dave Smith (1981)

The American Book of the Dead
Jim Barnes (1982)

Northbook
Frederick Morgan (1982)

The Floating Candles
Sydney Lea (1982)

Collected Poems, 1930–83
Josephine Miles (1983)

The River Painter
Emily Grosholz (1984)